The Tower on the
The Story of Haldon Bel
and the Palks of Haldon

by
Christopher Pidsley

ORCHARD PUBLICATIONS
2 Orchard Close, Chudleigh, Devon TQ13 0LR
Telephone: (01626) 852714

ISBN 9781898964827

Printed by
Hedgerow Print, Crediton, Devon EX17 1ES

i

The Palk Family Arms – 'God is my Guide'

The Story of Haldon Belvedere and the Palks of Haldon House

The story starts at a small farm known as Lower Headborough, just off the road that leads from Ashburton to Buckland in the Moor. It was here that Walter Palk (b.1691) brought up his three children, Walter, Robert and Grace. It was his second son Robert (b.1717) who was destined to achieve fame and amass a fortune. He was educated at the local grammar school from where he went up to Wadham College, Oxford in 1736. He was ordained in Exeter Cathedral in 1739, and proceeded to serve a curacy at Egloskerry and Launcells, just over the border in Cornwall, which at this time was part of the Diocese of Exeter. A few years later he confided in a friend that he was "starving in his curacy". His friend suggested he should seek service abroad and in due course he signed up as a chaplain in the navy. Some sources suggest that he received a recommendation from the Prime Minister, Sir Robert Walpole.

Lower Headborough Farm as it is today

After various adventures at sea while serving on a number of ships, he arrived in India in 1747. It was here he experienced a lucky break which would change the whole course of his life. The East India Company chaplain at Fort David had been recently dismissed, having had a public fracas with Robert Clive, who was later to become the celebrated 'Clive of India'. Palk was recruited to fill his place, having been recommended by Admiral Boscawen as "a very worthy and able divine".

Robert Palk as a young man *Maj. General Stringer Lawrence*

Before long, Palk met up with Major Stringer Lawrence (later Maj. Gen.) who had been appointed to raise an army to protect British trading interests, and prevent the French from gaining the upper hand. Stringer Lawrence recruited a five hundred strong battalion of foot soldiers and subsequently became known as 'The Father of the Indian Army'. It soon became clear that Palk was a shrewd judge of character, and he also demonstrated considerable skills in negotiating with the Indian princes. So it was that Lawrence the miltary strategist and Palk the diplomat, developed a very effective partnership. It is also recorded that Palk had "a gift for conciliation in disputes" and was often "sent to soften and manage Lawrence's warm and sudden temper"! In due course Palk was appointed as Paymaster and Quartermaster to Lawrence's army. After ten years Palk returned to England well rewarded for his services. He renounced his deacon's orders, and married Anne Vansittart, of Shottesbrook Park, Berkshire, sister of one of his colleagues in India who became Governor of Bengal.

In 1762 Palk was once more approached by the East India Company and persuaded to return to the Subcontinent to sort out various problems. On his return he was elected to the Council of the Company and was appointed as Governor of Madras. He was also given a number of other lucrative positions, including being Export Warehouse Keeper. This latter post enabled him to engage in a certain amount of trading on the side, sending spices to the Far East and importing silks and other goods for onward shipment to the west. He also traded in diamonds and coral. Records of the time suggest that, "The fortune with which he returned to England was not all derived from his official emoluments". A contemporary commentator also noted that, "whilst placing the interests of his employer first, Palk did not entirely neglect his own. Whilst he would not stoop to solicit gifts, he was very happy to receive them!"

An Estate in Devon and a Seat in Parliament
In 1767 he returned to his London home a very wealthy man. Shortly after his arrival he wrote to his friend William Goodland, back in India, "I am settled in a town house for at least three years and whenever anything offers to my liking, I shall make a purchase in the country. In this very expensive land it becomes necessary to get into a settled way of life as soon as possible". In common with a number of his contemporaries who had amassed a fortune in India, his ambition was to become a country gentleman. Returning to his native Devonshire he purchased the Manor of Tormohun, an estate of several hundred acres and the ancient homestead of Torwood Grange, just inland from the small fishing village of Tor Quay. However in this instance, his skills as a negotiator were not sufficient to persuade Sir George Cary of Torre Abbey, to sell him a couple of fields which would give him direct access to the sea and prevent any future development which would spoil his view!

Haldon House c 1790 as enlarged by Robert Palk

Whilst retaining his initial purchase, Palk decided to look elsewhere to fulfil his dream. Eventually he settled on Haldon House, in the parish of Dunchideock, which he purchased in 1769. This grand mansion was reputed to have been modelled on the original Buckingham House, later to become Buckingham Palace, erected for the Duke of Buckingham in 1703. Haldon House had been built between 1720 and 1735, and the estate eventually comprised some 11,500 acres lying on both sides of the Haldon Hills. The new owner set about enlarging the house and making substantial improvements. Richard Polwhele, in his *History of Devonshire,* notes that "there were formerly slopes and steps that led up to the hall door so that the offices below were underground. All this ascent Sir Robert Palk removed and laid open the offices by which the house appears one storey higher than before."

In addition to changes in the appearance of the house, Palk introduced elaborate furniture and paintings by prominent artists such as Rembrandt and Gainsborough, pride of place being occupied by a portrait of Maj. Gen. Stringer Lawrence, by Sir Joshua Reynolds. The grounds and parkland were landscaped with expert advice from Lancelot 'Capability' Brown. The spacious Pleasure Garden was stocked with many rare trees and shrubs; it incorporated a series of ornamental pools, the outlet from each forming a miniature waterfall with the stream finally flowing into a small lake.

Before long William Goodland received another letter from his old friend reporting that, "I have at last, near Exeter, pitched my tent – in a good house and very pleasant country, close to the road when in good time you land at Plymouth".

Palk soon took an interest in local affairs becoming M.P. for Ashburton. In Parliament he was a valued spokesman on matters relating to the Indian Subcontinent which at this time made a major contribution to the British economy. He was knighted in 1772 in recognition of his public service.

An Enduring Friendship

Stringer Lawrence had left India a year before Palk, but their friendship continued, and once Palk had settled on his Devonshire estate, Lawrence was a frequent visitor, if not a permanent guest. He was said to enjoy walks with his cocker spaniel on the 800ft Pen Hill, an ancient neolithic site above the house. Lawrence was invited to be godfather to Palk's first son who, along with all subsequent heirs, was given the name Lawrence. (A nightmare for anyone trying to piece together the family history!)

When Stringer Lawrence died in 1775 he left his not inconsiderable fortune, said to be between £50,000 and £80,000, to the Palk family. He was buried in Dunchideock Church, where there is a memorial to him on the north wall. There is also an elaborate memorial to him in Westminster Abbey which features the following epitaph written by Hannah Moore, a noted poet of the day, which reads thus:-

General Lawrence
Born to command, to conquer, and to spare,
As mercy mild, yet terrible as war,
Here Lawrence rests – the trump of honest fame
From Thames to Ganges has proclaimed his name:
In vain this frail memorial Friendship rears

Stringer Lawrence Memoral in Westminster Abbey

His dearest monument an Army's tears'
His deeds on fairer columns stand engraved
In Provinces preserved and cities saved.

When Dunchideock church was restored in 1892, his body, along with those of members of the Palk family, was reinterred in a simple grave in the chuchyard to the west of the tower. The details of this reinterment are recorded on plaque inside the church. The shared grave outside is marked with a single letter 'p', which is now hard to see.

The Building of the Belvedere

As a more dramatic tribute to his friend and benefactor, Palk built the70ft high Haldon Belvedere, (from the Italian bel videre—beautiful view). The tower

5

standing on the top of Penn Hill was completed in 1788. It is said that much of the material for the building of the three-sided tower came from the ruins of Sir George Chudleigh's original house, Place Barton, at Higher Ashton. Three-sided towers were very much in fashion at the time. The Duke of Cumberland had Shrub Hill Tower built at Windsor in 1757, and the Courtenays erected one on their estate at Powderham in 1773. Another, Severndroog Castle, had been built in 1784 on Shooters Hill, South London, to commemorate Sir William James, commander of the East India Company's maritime force in India.

Around the walls of the ground floor of the Belvedere Tower, there is a series of eulogy boards extolling Lawrence's virtues and achievements. The first board records that it is, "To the memory of Major General Stringer Lawrence who, for the space of twenty years, commanded the British armies in India; and by his superior genius, consummate skill, and unremitting exertion, with an inferior force, extinguished the power of France and restored the glory of the British name." The centre of the room is dominated by a life-size statue of Lawrence, dressed as a Roman general, a Coadestone copy of the marble original, which stands in the Foreign Office, formerly East India House. The Tower, as well as being built as a memorial, also served a practical purpose, being used for elaborate entertainment. The guests and liberal refreshments were transported from the house via a specially constructed carriage drive incorporating two bridges over public roads, both of which may still be seen. It is said that the bridges were built so the guests would not have to mix with the common people! After a visit by George III and Queen Charlotte, in 1789, the carriage drive became known as The King's Drive. Some sources suggest that George IV, who succeeded to the throne in 1820, was also entertained by the Palks.

The top bridge

The Belvedere c 1920

Lawrence as a Roman General

The lower bridge on the King's Drive

Sir Robert Palk died in1798 at the age of eighty one, and Worth, in his book *Devon Parishes,* says that "his touch seemed to turn everything to gold, he enriched his relatives his friends and his surroundings. He was an ancestor to look back on, a forefather of whom any family would be proud". Sadly of his six children, only two survived, Anne who married Sir Bouchier Wrey of Tawstock, and Lawrence (1766-1813). Lawrence's first marriage to Mary Bligh, daughter of the Earl of Darnley, was childless. When she died, he married Lady Dorothy Vaughan, the daughter of the Earl of Lisburn, of nearby Mamhead House. The third of their eight children, Elizabeth Malet Palk, married Sir Horace Beauchamp Seymour in 1818 and their fourth child Adelaide, married Frederick Spencer in 1854. Frederick Spencer's great grandson was Earl Spencer, father of Diana, Princess of Wales.

Returning to our story, Lawrence continued to modernise the estate, building the model farm complete with barns, stables, cowsheds, piggeries, granary, slaughterhouse, cider press and wagon and cart sheds. Machinery for various operations, including corn grinding and chaff cutting, was driven by an overshot waterwheel supplied by a reservoir on the hill above.

The Development of Torquay

In 1803 Lawrence began to develop the land still owned by the family in Torquay. In the event he only survived his father by fifteen years, dying in 1813 at the age of forty-seven. Following his death it became apparent that he had consumed a vast amount of the family fortune in a very short time! He was succeeded by his twenty year old son, Lawrence Vaughan (1793-1860), who pressed ahead with the development of Torquay, engaging in schemes most of which were financed by mortgages. It was a boom time for the town, as the wars on the continent necessitated an alternative holiday destination for the rich and famous. It was probably from this time that Torquay became known as the English Riviera. Today the Palk connection is still evident from many street names e.g Palk Street, Vansittart Road, Vaughan Parade, Lisburne Cresent and Haldon Road to name but a few. In 1832, an arch was built at the entrance to Palk Street, as an additional memorial to General Stringer Lawrence. The arch was demolished by Lloyds Bank in 1932, only for the Haldon Estates to insist that it was rebuilt. It was finally removed in 1962.

The most prestigious development, commissioned by Sir Lawrence Vaughan, was undoubtedly Hesketh Crescent, overlooking Meadfoot Beach and incorporating fifteen separate properties. It was designed by the brothers William and John Harvey and completed in 1848. It is said to be the finest crescent of houses west of Bath. Among many other developments, The Royal Hotel was enlarged and improved in order to cater "for families of the first distinction". Lawrence Vaughan may have been credited with many of the distinctive features of Torquay, but it was Dr Henry Beeke, one time Dean of Bristol, followed in 1833 by William Kitson the family banker, steward and solicitor, who were thought to have been the prime movers. Outside Kitson's former office is a blue plaque pronouncing him as, 'The Maker of Torquay'.

Hesketh Crescent, Torquay

Despite apparent success, there were acute financial problems in the background, such that in 1858, Lawrence Vaughan had to flee to the continent to escape his creditors. Percy Russell in his *History of Torquay,* describes Sir Lawrence Vaughan as "an incapable spendthrift". His son was so worried that he initiated legal steps to have his father certified as a lunatic! Matters were eventually sorted out with the setting up of a family trust. This move enabled Lawrence Vaughan to return to England to live out his days at 15, Hesketh Crescent where he died in 1860, aged sixty-seven. Over the years, in order to recoup some of the expense of maintaining Haldon House, it seems that it was often rented out. For example, back in 1827 *The Times* had noted that the Duke of Sussex was leasing Haldon House for the summer, 'in order to improve his health'.

Lawrence Vaughan's son, yet another Lawrence (1818-1883) was married to Maria Hesketh, only daughter of Sir Thomas Hesketh Bt., of Rufford Hall Lancashire. Following the death of his father, Lawrence continued with the development of Torquay. He chose to live at No 8, Hesketh Crescent, then called Osborne House, becoming in later years The Osborne Hotel. The hotel was a favourite venue for the rich and famous, a frequent guest being the Prince of Wales, the future Edward VII. It is said that during his visits he arranged for his mistress Lily Langtry to stay at a house nearby. This story would seem to be reflected in the fact that today the hotel restaurant is called 'Langtry's'. In the early days of the hotel, sea bathing from the beach below was strictly controlled and a local bye-law stated "No person of the male sex shall at any time bathe within 50 yards of a ladies bathing machine"!

In 1853 Lawrence moved from Osborne House to The Manor House, an impressive property, with views over the harbour, which he had had built on Lincombe Hill. Almost exactly one hundred years after Robert Palk had built Torquay's first harbour, his great grandson, Sir Lawrence, initiated the building of the Outer Harbour, protected by the Haldon Pier. This ambitious project cost £70,000. It provided safe anchorage for the increasing number of yachts and steamers, which arrived at the resort during the summer months. It was officially opened during the Torbay Royal Regatta in 1870. Sir Lawrence was at this time Commodore of the Yacht Club and the owner of the 280 ton schooner 'Gulnare', and a cutter, 'The Lancashire Witch', which he had had built at Teignmouth.

Another of his interests was the construction of the Teign Valley Railway Line, in which he invested £30,000 (see inside back cover). His hope was that the line would eventually provide transport for the various minerals, including copper, iron and lead, extracted on his land in the valley, to his port at Torquay. Unfortunately the price of minerals dropped and the line was destined to provide little return for the initial shareholders. It was opened as far as the Teign House Inn in 1882, but did not reach Exeter until 1903, owing to a shortage of capital. There were also

Chudleigh Station

10

engineering problems, as two tunnels were required between Dunsford and Ide. During the first half of the 20th century up to 500 tons of stone a day, extracted from the various quarries, was despatched from the Valley. One added benefit of the line was that it provided an alternative route between Exeter and Newton Abbot, when Brunel's exposed coastal route was impassable. The line was finally closed for passengers in 1958 and for goods traffic a few years later.

Great Rock Mine in the Teign Valley. Closed in 1969.

A peerage is followed by a deepening financial crisis

Lawrence counted Prime Minister Disraeli among his friends and in 1880 he was raised to the peerage, becoming the first Lord Haldon, in acknowledgement of his service to the government and his many local public works. Sadly his enhanced status could not hide the continuing financial mismanagement, not to mention reckless gambling. His gambling included what was described as "spider racing round a plate", a favourite pastime of the gentry. This involved placing marked spiders on a plate that was gradually heated; the last one off the plate was the winner! A few months before he died aged sixty-five, in 1883, Lawrence was declared bankrupt.

On the death of his father, Lawrence Hesketh (1846-1903) inherited the title. He had served in the Scots Fusiliers, during which time he had acquired the nickname 'Piggy', since Palk readily became Pork. He was a keen gambler and a member

The First Lord Haldon

of the Turf Club. His interest in horse racing may well have been stimulated by the proximity of the Haldon Racecourse at which the inaugural meeting had been held on 11th July 1769. For a time he owned a racehorse called 'Stormlight', but it brought him little success. Desperate for money, land and properties were gradually sold off, and in 1892 it was decided to put Haldon House on the market.

Lawrence Hesketh's son, Lawrence William (1869-1933), had watched the family fortune steadily evaporate and the family home sold. So in 1893 he sought some consolation by marrying the daughter of a colonel in the Imperial Russian Army, who was described as 'an actress and a dancer'! She was apparently a widow and thirteen years his senior. In a further effort to drown his sorrows, Lawrence William was noted for his lavish champagne parties in London, and the music hall singer George Leybourne was reputed to have written the song *Champagne Charlie* after attending one such party. Despite his parlous financial situation, at one point he endeavoured to set up a company to sell false teeth on an instalment plan and even to rent them out!! Not surprisingly, in 1902

Lawrence Hesketh, the 2nd Lord Haldon

Lawrence William complained that he was suffering from "a little excess of expenditure over income"! Lawrence Hesketh, the second Lord Haldon, apparently fell down some stairs on Christmas Eve 1903; this lead to the onset of pneumonia as a result of which he died aged forty-nine.

Shortly after inheriting the title, Lawrence William was declared bankrupt. In 1928, Lawrence William's wife, the actress and dancer, died and a year later he married Edith Castle. Before long he and his new wife were living in a boarding house in Brixton. The rent was £1 a week and it is said that they cooked on a stove at the end of the bed. Further tragedy was to follow, for in May 1930 it was reported that a

The 3rd Lord Haldon

newspaper boy had seen a lady fall over some cliffs at Brighton. The body, found wedged between boulders at the foot of Black Rock, was identified as that of Lady Haldon. Lawrence William was grief stricken. At the inquest, he said he had last seen her the day before, when she set off from the boarding house to change a library book. She had apparently been suffering from headaches and sleeplessness and an open verdict was recorded. Three years later, Lawrence William, the third Lord Haldon, died and was buried in the churchyard at Kenn.

An ignominious end

After all that had happened it is not surprising that the fourth Lord Haldon, Lawrence William's son, Lawrence Edward Broomfield (1896-1938), was a bit of a drifter. His father had described him as "hopeless". He was reported by *The Times* as having had a series of jobs, among them flax farmer, clerk, film actor, ship's cook and furniture salesman at Harrods! He was arrested on a number of occasions for theft and for obtaining money by false pretences. In 1926, the *Express and Echo* of 19th May reported that he was a missing person. He was described as thirty years old, five foot ten inches tall, with a long face, a rather long nose and a Charlie Chaplin moustache. He was also said to be a malarial subject of no fixed abode.

Shortly after inheriting the title in 1933 he was in London addressing envelopes during the day and working as a waiter in a hotel in Holborn in the evening. He even resorted to selling matches on the streets. In 1938 he was living in a bed-sit in the Kings Cross Road, his sole income fourteen shillings and eleven pence (75p), of which he had to pay ten shillings a week in rent. One day he was found collapsed on the steps of Westminster Hospital. He was admitted and a gastric ulcer was diagnosed. He died a few days later, following an operation, at the age of forty-two.

There is just one final twist in the story of the Palks. At Lawrence Edward's funeral it was reported that there were two 'widows' present, one of whom, Lizzie Ireland, claimed to have married the deceased in Scotland a few months earlier. *The Times* reported that this 'widow' stated she had given birth to a son who was the rightful heir to the title. An investigation showed that this had been an elaborate hoax. At the age of sixty-two, she had purchased an unwanted baby to support her claim! She was charged with conspiracy, concealing a birth, and causing a false entry to be made in the Register of Births and Deaths. She was sentenced to three years penal servitude.

After Lawrence Edward's death the title passed to his uncle The Hon Edward Arthur Palk who was the last baron. He only survived for five months and from him the baronetcy passed to his second cousin, William Lawrence Lancelot Palk and when he died in 1945, the title became extinct.

The Final Days of the House and Estate

After the Palks had finally abandoned Haldon House in 1892, it was acquired for Mr James Bannatyne from Ireland. Mr Bannatyne had inherited the Limerick Milling Company, and despite the fact that it was a loss making business, he had managed to sell it at a handsome profit. With the proceeds, he determined to achieve his life long ambition to become an English country gentleman, by taking up residence at Haldon House with his wife Gertrude, his son and two daughters. The purchase price of the house was said to be £46,000. Some years later, according to the sale catalogue produced in 1925, the Bannatynes were reputed to have spent nearly £100,000 modernising the property and its surroundings. Among other things, they made a major alteration to the appearance of the front elevation of the house, by constructing sweeping flights of steps up to the balcony, thus restoring the access to the original central front door. They also built the Clapham Lodge and provided impressive wrought iron gates at the start of the mile long drive.

Clapham Lodge, 1925

One of the early guests at the recently refurbished house was the celebrated inventor of wireless telegraphy, Guglielmo Marconi, who stayed on a number of occasions. He is reputed to have carried out some of his early experiments with wireless transmission from the Belvedere, to a receiver on Dartmoor. It is said that the gardener's boy, Harold Tothill, of Copse Cottage, was instructed to cut down the longest bamboo stems he could find, to support the aerials!

During the Bannatynes tenure, the house and grounds were the setting for elaborate social gatherings. Family photographs of the period record finely dressed ladies and gentlemen, enjoying picnics and games of tennis and cricket in the early years of the 20th century. In July 1911, the Bannatynes elder daughter married Ludovick Heathcote Amory, of Knightshayes Court, Tiverton. Sadly the idyllic life on the estate was soon overshadowed by the outbreak of the First World War, and the death of Mr Bannatyne on 18th October 1915. Less than a year later the news came from France that his son James had died on 14th May 1916, as a result of wounds received in battle. Before the conflict was finally over, his son-in-law was also dead.

The demolition men move in

Following the loss of her husband, her only son, and her son- in law, and the absence of most of the menservants at the War, Mrs Bannatyne saw no possibility of remaining at Haldon House. Over the next six or seven years, most of that which remained of the once great estate was gradually sold off in a series of auctions. However the house itself did not attract a buyer. By 1925 the house had deteriorated so badly, that it was eventually sold for demolition; the price, £8,500, which included just 36 acres of the surrounding land.

Haldon House c 1920

Over the next fifteen years most of the building was gradually demolished. Apparently much of the rubble was used to fill in marshland at Exmouth. All that remains today is the west wing, which originally incorporated the servant's quarters, the stables and coach houses. This last vestige of the once great house was later purchased by a couple who ran it as a guesthouse until 1963; it was then bought by a Mr and Mrs Martin who continued to run it as a guesthouse for a further ten years.

The Martins tell of regular encounters with a ghostly presence, thought to be a young servant girl who met a violent end. They also learned much about the goings on at the house from their old gardener whose family had had links stretching back many years. The gardener recalled being told that on the arduous coach journey down from London, the gentry would imbibe liberal quantities of alcohol. On arrival at the house they had to be carried inside and in the process gold coins would fall from their pockets which were eagerly gathered by the servants! The old gardener also spoke of the numerous staff employed in the house and in the grounds, among them four men whose main task was to sweep the mile long drive every day. Following the Martins there were two more owners before the

Preece family bought the property and turned it into the Lord Haldon Hotel in 1981. After twenty-five years the family sold it to a private buyer in 2006 and the business was linked to the Best Western Hotel Group. At the rear of the hotel a section of the original house is still privately owned. Today if you visit the hotel after a long dry spell, you can still see on the lawns the outline of parts of the old house. Fittings from the ballroom were incorporated into the ballroom at Exeter's Thistle Hotel (formerly the Rougement Hotel). A fine pair of mahogany doors were acquired by the Imperial Hotel also in Exeter, and other items from the mansion found their way into various houses in Dunchideock! The Chapel, built in 1876 as a memorial to the third son of the first Lord Haldon, Walter George Palk, who died at the age of twenty-six, was near the main house. It was never consecrated and has been turned into a private residence known as Lawrence House. Some of the original furniture and fittings were taken to Clifton College Chapel, Bristol.

The Lord Haldon Hotel as it is today

Any old iron? Bedsteads form a field boundary

The tunnel under the road leading to the kitchen garden

The nearby range of farm buildings gradually fell into disrepair and in 1974 they were converted into an attractive series of properties now known as Tower Court. On the slopes leading up to the Tower, a field boundary has been created using thirty or forty iron bedsteads wired together, and one assumes they must have come from the servants quarters when much of the house was demolished.

In the 1920s the Pleasure Garden, with its mature trees and extensive water features culminating in the small lake, was sold off, and a fine private house, known as Haldon Grange, was built to take advantage of the landscaped setting. At the time of writing the Pleasure Garden is opened to the public in the early summer through the National Gardens Scheme. The walled kitchen garden, once approached by a tunnel under the road, was also sold together with the attractive Gardeners Cottage, which has since been extended.

Teas at the Tower

The Tower and top bridge in the 1920s

At the time of the outbreak of the First World War, the Tower on the hill, was shut up. In 1917, the Dale Family from the Midlands expressed an interest in purchasing it but later withdrew. After the final sale of the House in 1925, the Tower was bought by a syndicate for £300. At this time the Tower was obscured from view by trees, only the tops of the turrets being visible. The timber was sold and felled by the timber merchants Bartlett and Bayliss of North Devon. Apparently, while in the ownership of the syndicate occasional 'pyjama parties' were held at the Tower. It must have been a rather draughty venue! A daughter of Mr Bartlett married a Mr Smith and she then became the owner of the tower.

In 1933, the interest of Mrs Annie Dale was rekindled and she eventually purchased the tower from Mrs Smith for £650. Together with her two sons, Cyril and Edward, she opened the tower to the public, establishing a tea room for the many visitors. Local people remember Mrs Dale presiding over the operation in a variety of very large floppy hats! There was, apparently, a third brother who was married and lived at Ide.

During the World War Two the Tower was taken over by the army as a strategic observation post. In the years following the War, the Dale brothers returned to live in the Tower. On the days when it was open to the public one brother would sit at a table at the bottom of the drive with a roll of tickets while the other would show visitors around. On one occasion a local scout troop held a night exercise, the object of which was to reach the Tower without being spotted by their leaders As they made their way through the undergrowth a group was caught in the beam of a torch. There stood one of the Dales with a roll of threepenny tickets!

Living conditions in the Tower must have been very spartan, as there was no electricity or water supply, and the toilet was an ivy-clad privy in the trees. The only heating was provided by an open fire on each floor, with

The Tower in need of repair

the chimneys in one of the corner towers. The story is told that when a sweep from Christow came to sweep one of the chimneys in the 1930s he was mystified for, despite his careful calculations, the brush failed to appear at the top. Further investigation revealed that the chimney was a spiral! In the latter years Calor Gas was used for heating and cooking.

Rescue and Restoration

Over the years the fabric of the Tower progressively deteriorated, it was struck by lightning in 1960 and during a gale in 1990 three windows were blown out. Cyril Dale died in1990 and, just before he died in 1994, the remaining brother, Edward, transferred ownership of the Tower to a charitable trust, charged with maintaining the Tower as a memorial to General Stringer Lawrence. This initiative came none too soon for by this time the roof was in imminent danger of collapse.

One of the Dale brothers on the roof before restoration

The roof during restoration

The Stringer Lawrence Trust arranged for the Devon Historic Buildings Trust to restore the Tower and manage it. With a substantial grant from English Heritage and additional finance from Devon County Council, Teignbridge District Council, Exeter City Council and Devon Historic Buildings Trust, a major restoration project was carried out in 1995, the initial estimate for the work being £390,000. On 20th April 1996, the Tower was reopened by the architectural historian Lucinda Lambton. The final cost of the project amounted to over £450,000.

During the restoration various archaeological excavations were undertaken nearby. These revealed evidence of postholes and pits dating back to the early and middle Neolithic period, 3500-2500 B.C. Over four hundred examples of worked flints, including many arrowheads were found, and amongst the pottery were some of the earliest examples of ceramics unearthed in Britain.

The self catering apartment

Today the Tower is licensed for civil ceremonies and available for hire for other events. It so happened that the groom at the first ceremony to be conducted at the Tower was the grandson of Mrs Bessie Smith who owned the building in the early 1930s. Also available for hire is the fully furnished, twin bedded, self-catering apartment on the top floor, which boasts unrivalled views. Mains water and electricity have been introduced and the outside privy is no longer the only convenience! The Tower is currently open to the public on summer Sunday afternoons and Bank Holidays from February to October and from its lofty vantage point, the vast estates which once belonged to the Palks may be surveyed.

As for the farmer's son from Ashburton, his family name is perpetuated by 'The Palk Arms' at Hennock and by a street in Torquay. Thousands of miles away, at the scene of his initial influence and success, the Palkonda Hills near Madras are named after him, and the channel separating the southern tip of India from Sri Lanka is called the Palk Strait.

The Palk Arms, Hennock c 1900

The Palk Arms, 2000

So in the middle of the last century the sun finally set not only on the British Empire in India, but also on the Palks of Haldon House.

In her book *The Vanished Houses of South Devon*, Rosemary Lauder recalls that country folk of Devon have a saying "Rags to riches and back to rags in three generations". From relative obscurity, this branch of the Palk family rose to great prominence and acquired enormous wealth, only to end up with massive debt and embroiled in scandal. In a world concerned about national and personal debt, perhaps the story of *The Tower on the Hill* is something of a cautionary tale.

The Tower on the Hill

PALK FAMILY SYNOPSIS

Robert Palk (1717-1798)
Son of Walter Palk of Lower Headborough Farm Ashburton.
Educated at local Grammar School and Wadham College,Oxford.
Ordained at Exeter Cathedral 1839; curate at Egloskerry in Cornwall.
As naval chaplain sailed to India 1747; employed by the East India Company and worked with General Stringer Lawrence.
Returned to U.K. 1757; married Anne Vansittart 1761; returned to India 1762; appointed Governor of Madras.
Left India 1767 a very wealthy man; bought Torwood Grange Torquay, then bought Haldon House 1772.
Member of Parliament for Ashburton and knighted 1772.
Built Belvedere 1788 in memory of Stringer Lawrence.
Died 1798 aged 81.

Lawrence Palk (1766-1813)
Married Mary Bligh 1789, daughter of the Earl of Darnley, who died childless 1791.
Married Lady Dorothy Vaughan 1792, daughter of the Earl of Lisburne of Mamhead; inherited 1798; established the 'model' farm.
Began to develop land at Torquay and made improvements to the harbour.
Died 1813 aged 47.

Lawrence Vaughan Palk (1793-1860)
Inherited in 1813 at age of 20.
Married Anna Eleanor Wrey 1815, daughter of Sir Bourchier Wrey of Tawstock.
Prime developer of Torquay, including Hesketh Crescent in1848.
Experienced financial problems and fled to the Continent; returned to live at Hesketh Crescent where, died 1860 aged 67.

Lawrence Palk (1818-1883)
Married Maria Hesketh 1845 daughter of Sir Thomas Hesketh of Rufford Hall, Lancashire; inherited in 1860.
Continued development of Torquay; constructed Haldon Pier costing £70,000 completed in 1870.
Invested £30,000 in Teign Valley Railway Line (reached Teign House Inn in 1882 and Exeter 1903).
Created Lord Haldon 1880; bankrupt 1883.
Died 1883 aged 65.

Lawrence Hesketh Palk (1846-1903)
Second Lord Haldon; married Constance Barrington 1868; inherited the title and very little else 1883.
Sold Haldon House (previously rented out) in 1892.
Died in 1903 aged 57.

Lawrence William Palk (1869-1933)
Third Lord Haldon; married Lidiana Crezencia an actress and dancer in 1893 (who died 1928); inherited in 1903.
Married Edith Castle in 1929, she died in 'the Brighton tragedy' 1930.
Died 1933 aged 64.

Lawrence Edward Broomfield Palk (1896-1938)
Fourth Lord Haldon; inherited 1933.
Died 1938 penniless in Westminster Hospital aged 42.

Title passed to Lawrence Edward's great uncle Hon Edward Arthur Palk, he was the last baron; died 1939 aged 85. The last Baronet was William Lawrence Lancelot Palk. Died 1945 aged 69.

Bibliography

Around and about the Haldon Hills Chips Barber (1982)

Chudleigh - a Chronicle Anthony Crockett (1985)

Devon W.G.Hoskins (1954)

Travels in Georgian Devon 1798-1800 Vol.1 Rev John Swete

A History of Devonshire Richard Powhele 1793-1806

A Historical Survey of Torquay A.C.Ellis

A History of Torquay Percy Russell (1960)

A Guide to Torquay 1818

Haldon Belvedere – A Short History. Devon Historic Buildings Trust

This Sceptred Isle Christopher Lee p.377-381 (1997)

The Bannatyne Papers. A report on the Palk Manuscripts complied by
   H.M.Manuscript Commission. West Country Studies Library.

Vanished Houses of South Devon, Rosemary Lauder (1997)

Various newspaper cuttings in West Country Studies Library

Notes from the Dunchideock W.I. Local History Project

Descriptions from the 1918 and 1925 Sale Catalogues

Notes provided by the late Michael Preece of the Lord Haldon Hotel.